Starting your own Coffee Shop

Opening & Running a Successful Coffee Business

Jessica Simms

Starting your own Coffee Shop

Copyright © 2018

ISBN: 9781977036629

Warning and Disclaimer

Publisher Contact

Skinny Bottle Publishing

books@skinnybottle.com

Introduction 1

Chapter 1 5

The Business Plan 5

Chapter 2 15

Starting Expenses 15

Chapter 3 25

Menu, Products, and Services 25

Chapter 4 33

Branding and Identity 33

Chapter 5 37

Location 37

Chapter 6 41

Design 41

Chapter 7 49

Brewers and Grinders 49

Chapter 8 57

Making It Official 57

Chapter 9 61

Day-to-Day Operations 61

Chapter 10 67

Marketing 67

Chapter 11 71

Turning a Profit 71

Introduction

Many people dream of one day owning their own coffee shop. For most, though, this goes no further than an idea of something they'd like to do, someday, if they could find the time or money. They don't picture this dream ever becoming reality, usually because they don't think they can afford it or are afraid to make the leap from their current career to attempt to become a small business owner.

Owning a coffee shop is hard work; pretty much everybody agrees on that point. But that doesn't mean you should give up on your dream—if it's what you truly want to do. Before you take any steps toward opening your own coffee shop, that's the first thing you should make sure you're sure about. The number one reason so many new businesses fail is that the owner wasn't prepared for the reality of small business ownership. A coffee shop, especially, is an easy business to romanticize. For many people, owning a business means being their own boss and earning a huge profit. While that can be true, it also means putting in long hours, dealing with angry staff or customers, and other difficulties that you likely don't envision when you picture owning a café.

Most of the successful business owners put in 50-60 hours a week (and sometimes more), often working more than five days a week. It is not uncommon for the opening staff of a coffee shop to arrive at work at 5 a.m., sometimes even earlier if the café also bakes their own pastries. While you can hire a staff to work the hours you'd rather not, as the owner you'll be responsible for making sure they're trained correctly and representing your shop the way you want them to—and for disciplining them if they don't. There is also a lot of work involved in owning a coffee shop that has nothing to do with preparing drinks or interacting with customers. Placing orders, paying invoices, and analyzing sales are just some of the additional tasks that owners have to contend with beyond the typical work of a barista.

If you've seriously considered all these factors and are still excited by the idea of owning your own coffee shop, your very first step of the process should be to pick your opening date. It can be in six months or six years, and you may end up changing it a dozen times before you actually open, but picking a date will give you a target to shoot for and let you establish a timeline for what you need to do before you can get there. Be realistic with your date; consider both your personal financial health and your current life situation.

The chapters that follow in this book will give you an overview of what you need to know before diving into owning your own coffee shop. It will start from the planning stages and take you through the process of opening. By the end, you should have a

complete picture of just what it takes to open your own shop—
and to have it succeed in the long term.

Chapter 1

The Business Plan

Whatever kind of business you plan to start, writing a business plan should be the first step that you take. You can think of the business plan as the roadmap for your future company. In it, you'll outline the details of how you will start the business, what its intended purpose and goals will be, and how you'll bring it to into profitability. While a business plan won't be a requirement for you to start your company unless plan on applying for loans or securing investors, companies that take the time to write out a business plan tend to grow 30% faster than those that choose to skip this step and have a generally greater chance of long-term success. Especially if you have never owned or run a company before, a business plan is a very good idea to make sure you start off right.

The broadest definition of a business plan is a document that spells out exactly what your vision is for your business, including who you expect to have as your main customer base, how you plan to grow your business, who your competitors will be, and how you will make a profit. If you are applying for loans or seeking out investors, you will need to write out a formal business plan, which includes information on things like your corporate structure and management team. If the business plan is just for your own purposes, though, you can tailor the document to suit your specific needs, focusing on the operational aspects of the business.

The good news is that even formal business plans are generally shorter today than they were in the past; writing one doesn't have to be a daunting or arduous task. If you're only writing it for your own in-house use, it can be as short as one page or as long as you need it to be. Start with the sections you know how to describe and let it grow organically as you figure out more about what your business will look like.

You should think of your business plan as a dynamic document that continues to change as you learn about the industry and where you'll fit within it. Don't stop updating your business plan once you're open, either; as your business grows, so too should your business plan grow and change to reflect the current state of your company. If you do need to print the document to submit to a bank, grant, or investor, think of it as a snapshot of your business as it exists at that point in time. Never think of it as finished, or hesitate to change it to reflect new information or business practices. The business plan, if written correctly, should be your guide for the entire life of your business.

There are many different forms of business plans. At a minimum, your plan should include information on your company strategy, basic projections of your sales, costs, and cash flow, metrics and milestones that you'll use to track your success, products and services offered by the company, and a schedule for reviewing the business plan in the future. There are other sections that can

STARTING YOUR OWN COFFEE SHOP

optionally be included, as well. The sections described in the remainder of this chapter are generally the ones you'll need to include when you're opening a coffee shop, but remember that every business is different. If a different format or collection of sections will better suit your needs, use those instead; there is no one right way to write your plan, just like there's no one right way to run a company.

If you're still not sure what to write even after reading through this chapter, there are several resources online for getting ideas or help. One great place you might want to check is the website www.BPlans.com. Search here for "coffee" and you'll find sample business plans for a variety of different scenarios, including a sit-down coffee house, a coffee kiosk, a roasting operation, and more.

Products and Services

This is a section that is integral to all business plans, whether they're for internal or external use. It is in many ways the core of any good business plan because it explains broad operational details like the problem your company solves, how it solves it, and what you're trying to ultimately achieve with your company. For a coffee shop that's looking for outside financial investments, the main thing you'll want to clarify in this section is exactly what makes you different from the other coffee options in your area. If you're doing something that's not common in your area, like a slow bar or an in-house roaster, this is information that should be front and center. Even if there's nothing you can easily point to as differentiating you from other coffee shops, though, you should figure out what will make your business stand out, whether it's a certain atmosphere, a specific target demographic, or some other detail of your operation.

The Products and Services section of your business plan is also where you'll investigate your local competition. This is especially important for a coffee shop. In 2016, there were over 55,000 coffee shops in the United States alone, up from around 52,000 in 2013. This number doesn't include other more general businesses where customers can get a cup of coffee, either, like breakfast restaurants and gas stations. When you evaluate your competition, you should look at anywhere in your area that customers can buy coffee. If you also plan to be a roaster (or will sell bagged beans) you may also want to look at grocery stores in your area if they sell specialty coffee. If your local grocers only sell ground Folgers and the like, it's not as important to consider them as competition.

Looking at the list above it can seem like there's a daunting amount of competition in the coffee landscape. Coffee is a popular enough beverage that a new shop that does things well will be able to succeed, even if there are already multiple coffee shops operating in your area. It does mean you need to pay extra attention to the competition section of your business plan, though, because you'll need to establish a context for yourself of what other options are available to your customers. You may even find that looking at what does and does not exist already in your area will change your thoughts about what kinds of things you want to offer, or which neighborhoods you look at for your store. At the very least, gauging your competition will help you know what to expect and how to target your marketing. Evaluating your competitors is also especially important if you plan to submit the document for funding since it's something any investors will want to see you've considered.

Target Market

This is another section that should be considered a necessity for all business plans. It is where you'll describe the kinds of customers you expect to get. You should consider both geography and demographics in this section. Understanding who is most likely to patronize your establishment will be a great benefit in outlining your marketing and sales strategies.

The Target Market section of your business plan is one that's likely to go through many changes, both before and after your opening day. If you're writing your business plan before you've obtained a location, this section will likely be vague and mostly centered on demographics like gender, age, or profession. Once you know your location (or at least the general neighborhood) you should also consider the area—whether it's a residential or commercial district, for example, as well as what other businesses and attractions are nearby. Going through this step will also help you to refine your expected hours of operation and peak sales times.

Once you do open, make sure that you refine this section to reflect your actual sales figures and customer base. Keeping a close eye on your customer flow and how it changes from day to day and month to month will help you to better anticipate necessary changes to your staffing, hours, or inventory.

Marketing and Sales Plan

This is another important section of any business plan. It is a place to discuss, in a broad and general sense, how sales will be handled in your company, along with the advertising strategies you'll use to generate more of those sales. While sales and marketing are inextricably linked, you should consider each individually in this section, as well, along with thinking about the ways in which they inter-relate. On the sales side of things, this means establishing your pricing and anticipated daily and weekly volume. On the marketing side, consider what methods you'll use to reach your ideal potential customers. If you plan to offer promotional deals like punch cards or other loyalty discounts, this would be the section to discuss it.

Financial Plan

The Financial Plan will be like the Marketing and Sales Plan in that it will be a chance to examine your projected financials. The main difference between the Financial Plan and the Marketing and Sales sections is that the Financial Plan will deal with actual figures and numerical projections based on your estimated prices. Like the sections above, this is a necessary component of any successful business plan.

When your coffee shop is in its planning stages, this is the section where you'll figure out how much money you need to get started, and how you plan to obtain that money. If you're using the business plan to apply for funding, note any existing funds that you'll be using to supplement the money you're requesting. Include personal savings and any loans or investors you've already secured.

The Financial Plan is also where you'll include information on any money that will be coming in or going out on a regular basis. In the planning stages, you should draft an estimated cash flow and profit/loss statement for your first year of operation. Once the business is open, update your business plan frequently to reflect your actual figures regarding sales and costs. Don't forget about your own financial situation either. While you won't need to include this in external business plans, it's a helpful thing to include on internal plans, especially if you'll be the sole owner/operator. Determine how you'll separate your personal financials from those of the business and how you'll stay financially solvent while you wait for your business to reach profitability.

Metrics for Success

The final section that will be equally important on both internal and external business plans is your Milestones or Metrics section. While it can go by a variety of different names, the underlying intent is always the same: laying out, in detailed and concrete terms, how you will measure success at different stages of your business' life. These can be defined by a numerical profit benchmark, a level of growth expressed as a percentage, or some other attribute. The important thing is that this benchmark is precise and achievable.

As part of your Metrics section, you'll also want to determine what your coffee shop's break-even point will be. This is the stage at which the business becomes profitable and will vary from business to business depending on your start-up and operational expenses.

If there are multiple individuals at the ownership or management level within your business, you'll likely find it helpful to indicate who will be responsible for reaching the outlined benchmarks. Give yourself a due date or deadline that you want to reach your goals by. You can always change these details later down the line but having a firm deadline in mind (and someone who feels pressure to meet it) will help your business to feel more tangible.

Review Schedule

This is something you will typically only see included on in-house business plans; you can omit this section when you're preparing your document for outside eyes. It also does not need to be a long, written-out section. In fact, it can be as simple as a couple sentences specifying the next time you plan to review the business plan, along with notes to yourself about any specific areas of the plan that you want to make sure to return to.

How frequently you review your business plan is entirely up to your personal needs. In the planning stages, you will likely want to revisit your business plan every couple of months at the very least, and probably more like every couple of weeks, since new information will be more likely to alter your plans. Once you're open, coming back to the business plan once or twice per year should be sufficient.

Executive Summary

This is something that you'll only need to include in business plans that you'll be submitting to outsiders for funding, but it is necessary for business plans designed with that context in mind.

You can think of this as your company at a glance. It includes a brief description of the business plan itself, including any highlights, as well as an overview of the problem your coffee shop is intended to solve and how you'll solve it. It should also give some basic information about your target market and prospective financial data, as well as profiles of your management team and their qualifications to run a coffee shop.

In many cases, the Executive Summary will be written last, using the information you work out in the rest of business plan to create it. The Executive Summary should be punchy and compelling. Don't go into too much detail; that's what the rest of the business plan is for. The goal of the Executive Summary is to prepare the reader for the information contained in the rest of the document and to draw them into reading it and being interested in it.

Company Overview

This is another aspect of the business plan that you'll only need if you intend to submit the plan for funding; if the plan is only for in-house use, you can choose whether you feel like you need it. The main feature of the Company Overview is typically the mission statement, which can be a beneficial thing to write since it helps you to clarify your concept and express it in a single concise sentence.

If you are using your business plan for external purposes, the Company Overview will also include a summary of the company's structure, such as the ownership information and legal structure (e.g. whether it's an LLC, a partnership, a non-profit, etc.). Once your coffee shop is open and running, you should also include information about the location and the history of the company in this section.

Management Team

This is a more detailed exploration of the information you'll include in the Company Overview about the individuals in charge of the coffee shop, both at the organizational and operational level. Like the Company Overview, it's only necessary if your business plan is for external use.

If your coffee shop will be a partnership, co-op, or otherwise will have multiple individuals at the management level, include a section for each member if the team. If you're starting a coffee shop as the sole owner/operator, this will be a very short section of the document. Resist the temptation to pad it with unnecessary information. Simply state your background in either business or coffee and what makes you the right person for the job. While you should emphasize your strengths, you also want the business plan to provide a realistic picture of your company. Point out any gaps in your knowledge or experience, as well as how you plan to fill in those gaps. While your strengths and qualifications are what will ultimately help you to secure funding, pointing out your weaknesses shows a level of self-awareness that investors will appreciate.

Chapter 2

Starting Expenses

The amount of start-up capital that you'll need to open a coffee shop varies widely depending on factors like what menu items and services you offer and the location of your shop. For a coffee kiosk, stand, or food truck, the start-up expenses can be anywhere from $50,000 to $100,000. For a coffee shop with a seating area, the range can go as high as $250,000; if you want seating and a drive-thru, you should expect to spend about $200,000 to $300,000.

If you've been saving up to open your business for a while, you may have that much—or at least a significant percentage of it—set aside in an account. For most people, though, getting enough money together to cover all your initial costs can feel a bit overwhelming. If you have wealthy friends or family members, you can ask them to invest in your business; barring this, however, you'll be looking at outside sources for funding. Many new owners immediately look at small business loans to fill in the financial gaps. This may be the best choice for you, but it is often not your only option.

Check with your local Small Business Association or Chamber of Commerce for grants or seed loans your coffee shop might qualify for. Some cities will give you a certain percentage of your opening expenses if you open your shop in an underserved neighborhood. While this could be a risk, it could also be an opportunity to be on the front edge of the area's economic revitalization. You could also check to see if your city has a small business incubator or other organization aimed at connecting prospective owners with interested investors.

Before you start looking at potential funding sources, though, you want to make sure you have as accurate an estimate as possible of how much money you'll need to start the kind of coffee business you want in the location that you're targeting. The sections that follow in this chapter will go through the various expenses you should consider as you're budgeting for your new business.

Equipment and fixtures

Depending on the quantity and nature of the equipment you want to buy for your coffee shop, you may need to budget anywhere from $15,000 to $50,000 all told. You can cut down on this expense by looking for used rather than new equipment, though you should only do this with equipment that is familiar enough to you that you'll be able to tell if there are any problems (and ideally able to fix them when they arise) or you may end up spending more in the long run on repairs and replacements.

Your espresso machine will likely be the most expensive piece of equipment in your shop. Most machines that are suitable for use in a coffee shop will run in the $5,000 to $15,000 range; a brand new four-group machine from a major brand can cost upwards of

$20,000. While you may be able to find machines for less, this is one area of your shop you don't want to skimp on. You can't make good espresso and steamed milk unless you have a good machine; essentially, it will set the quality standard for your entire shop.

The other café-specific equipment you'll need is far less costly by the piece, though you should budget an additional $5,000-$15,000 for it all told. Expect to spend a minimum of $3,000 on grinders. Commercial drip brewers typically cost between $1,000 and $2,000 a piece; while other common equipment like hot water towers, commercial blenders, and manual brewers costs less per item, most coffee shops will spend an additional $1,000-$3,000 on these items.

It's also likely you'll need some more general equipment. You'll want a minimum of two refrigerators: a small one to keep near the espresso machine for ingredients you want close at hand, and a larger fridge for holding extra milk or food. If your location wasn't set up as a restaurant before, there are some basic things you'll need to install to be up to health code standards. A three-part sink is a requirement for restaurants in most states; you'll also need to have a sink near the espresso machine for rinsing pitchers, as well as a dedicated mop sink somewhere in the back. If there is no filtration system on the water, you'll need to install one at least on the lines going to your brewers. Other commonly needed fixtures include pastry cases, customer-facing refrigerators, freezers for pastry back-stock, and food preparation equipment, which can range from toaster ovens to industrial ovens, depending on what you plan to offer.

Furnishings and décor

This is one place where buying used is often a great way to cut back on expenses. How much total you'll need to spend will depend largely on the size of your space. For a kiosk or food truck, you may only need to spend a few hundred dollars for some paint and exterior signage; a full café with seating will need to budget significantly more. Don't forget to include the cost of any interior construction.

POS

The acronym POS stands for Point of Sale and refers to your system for accepting customer money. For a coffee shop, a tablet-based POS system should work just fine. ShopKeep and Square are the most popular options; Square even has a free version that might have enough features to suit your needs. While you will need to budget around $500-$1,500 for the initial expense of hardware like the cash register, receipt printer, and credit card swiper, a modern POS system is far more affordable than it was ten years ago.

Inventory

How much inventory you want to have on hand when you open will depend on several factors. The size and nature of your shop are some of the most important considerations. If you run a coffee truck or kiosk, you'll be more limited in how much inventory you can keep on hand unless you have an external storage space. Buying larger quantities of non-perishable items can lower your per-item cost, if you have the space for it, but will also be a larger one-time investment.

Consider all items that will need to be periodically replenished when you plan your inventory. While you'll go through paper to-go cups faster than ceramic mugs, for here dishes will eventually break. You should maintain a back stock in the shop, so they can be replenished as needed. Your needs will vary depending on your exact set-up and menu, but the most common inventory items for a coffee shop are listed below.

Non-perishable items

Non-perishable items are things that you can keep in stock indefinitely without worrying about it expiring. The only limit on how much back stock you can keep on hand is the size of your storage area. This gives you the chance to buy these items in bulk for a lower per-item cost. You may want to order some of these items well in advance of your opening, especially if you're using branded cups or napkins since you can take these to promotional events prior to opening day to start spreading the word.

Paper products: Hot cups and lids, cold cups and lids, cup jackets, stir sticks, cup carriers, straws, pastry bags, pastry paper, to-go containers, plastic silverware, napkins, saran wrap, coffee bags (if selling whole bean/ground coffee)

Dishware: Mugs, saucers, demitasse cups, plates, silverware

Cleaning products: Grindz tablets (or another grinder cleaner), Cafiza, Urnex (or other coffee brewer cleaner), sanitizer solution, cleaning chemicals, replacement mop heads, cloth towels, paper towels, hand soap

Operational supplies: Receipt paper, office supplies (pens for signing, pads for notes, etc.), shot glasses (for pouring shots)

Semi-perishable items

There are quite a few items in a typical coffee shop's inventory that won't last forever but have a shelf life that can be measured in months or even years. This means you can buy these items in advance so they're ready to go when you open. Once your shop's operational, you'll also have more flexibility with the frequency and size of your orders.

Drink supplies: Tea (bags, boxed Chai mixes, Matcha powder), bottled syrups and sauces, sugar and sweetener packets, bulk sugar, chocolate powder, boxed milks (soy, hemp, almond, etc.), green coffee beans (if roasting), bottled beverages

Food items: Frozen pastries, frozen breakfast sandwiches, ready to make oatmeal, packaged snacks (granola bars, bagged chips, etc.)

Retail items: Vacuum-sealed beans, mints, and candies

Perishable Goods

Items that will go bad in a matter of days are the trickiest to manage when it comes to your inventory. You're more likely to place orders and get deliveries multiple times per week. Buying in bulk is less of an option; instead, you want to try to anticipate your sales and order exactly as much as you need to reduce waste. You will likely want to wait to receive your first order of these items until shortly before opening day.

Examples: Milk, roasted coffee, fresh fruit, yogurt, pre-made juices, food purchased through vendors (baked goods, pre-made salads, and sandwiches, etc.)

Operating expenses

You shouldn't expect your coffee shop to be an overnight success. To give yourself some time to get going, you should have enough to cover at least your first six months of operating expenses in the bank on opening day. If you end up reaching a point of profitability before that, you can always put the money towards another expense, or save it in case of an emergency or rainy day.

Your monthly operating expenses are everything you must pay to keep your doors open. This includes utilities like gas, electric, water, and sewage, as well as your mortgage or lease payment and services like garbage collection and insurance payments. If you took out loans to start your business, include those payments in your monthly budget. Also, include any recurring payments for services like Wi-Fi. Don't forget to include a section in your budget for maintenance and repairs.

Even if you're the sole owner/operator, you'll likely want to hire at least a small staff of baristas. Figure out how many hours of work you'll need from employees each week and include that in your budget, as well. Don't forget about the other expenses that come along with having employees, like workman's compensation benefits and payroll taxes.

Other start-up expenses

Every license and permit that you must apply for to open your business will carry an associated fee. The exact amount will vary depending on where you are. Each one individually is usually not expensive, but they can add up if you don't account for them in your budget. You should also obtain insurance for your business prior to opening. In many places this is a requirement; even if it's not, it's a good idea.

Finally, after you've identified all your known costs, look at the total that you've come up with and add on an extra 10-20% for unanticipated expenses. This gives you a cushion in case something goes awry during the building, or if equipment and supplies end up costing more than you thought they would. You don't want to get your shop 95% complete and end up failing because you ran out of money at the end. If you don't end up using it, you can put it into other aspects of the business, like extra inventory or marketing.

Personal finances

When you're wrapped up in figuring out how you'll start your business, it can be easy to forget about your own living expenses. This is an important thing to consider, however. You're going to be devoting most of your time to the business once it opens, and you aren't likely to make enough to pay yourself for your efforts for at least the first few months. Having savings to live from while you get your coffee shop off the ground will make sure you can keep food on your table and a roof over your head.

Figure out how much you need to live each month. A good rule of thumb is that you should have at least enough saved up to cover your personal expenses for six months. By this point, your coffee shop should be bringing in enough profit to pay yourself at least enough to survive.

Throughout the life of your business, you should keep your personal financials as separate from the company's financials as possible. Forming an LLC is one way to protect your assets in case something goes awry down the line. The cardinal rule of starting a new company is that your investment should never put your personal livelihood at risk. Make sure you don't lose sight of yourself as you're gearing up to open your coffee shop.

Chapter 3

Menu, Products, and Services

In many ways, figuring out what items and services your coffee shop will offer is the step of the planning process that really brings your idea to life. It is also one of the most important steps since much of the rest of the planning will depend on what kind of things you're serving. Figuring out your menu will help you better clarify your shop's identity, and can inform the design. It may even help you decide which neighborhood your shop will belong in.

Deciding on your menu doesn't have to mean coming up with every drink recipe or setting prices, although those are things you'll do at some stage of the process. To start with, though, you should think more in broad strokes. Start by figuring out what kinds of brewing methods you want to offer. Do you want to have a slow bar with Chemex and pour-over stations, or do you want to focus more on espresso-based drinks? Will you create your own in-house roasts and blends, or will you serve another company's beans—and if that's the case, whose? Using beans from a local roaster can enhance your credibility and bring in customers you might not have gotten otherwise.

One thing you absolutely should do at this stage is to learn everything you possibly can about your product. Taste a wide range of coffees from different regions and roasters to figure out what you like. Experiment with different brewing and roasting practices in your home, and attend any coffee events that are happening in your area, whether those are cuppings or latte art competitions. Seek out organizations like the SCAA and Barista's Guild; even if you don't join, they can be a great source for the latest news on the coffee industry, whether that's the most recent Cup of Excellence winner or a disease outbreak that will affect beans from a certain region. If you've never worked professionally with coffee before, it may be a good idea to get a part-time job at a local coffee shop. This will not only give you a better sense of how a coffee shop functions in the real world but will also let you start making connections with baristas in your area, something that will be very important for both hiring and marketing down the line.

Unless you have someone else on the team who will be running the day-to-day operations of the coffee shop, you as the owner should be the best barista on the staff. You should know your product intimately and be able to train someone with no barista experience to make the drinks correctly. You may find it helpful to not only join an organization like the SCAA but to go through the steps of getting certified. While this will be an extra expense it will pay great dividends in your knowledge and ability to best provide quality drinks for your customers. Being SCAA certified can also be valuable when you're looking for investors, as it shows them you have a vetted knowledge of coffee.

As you're figuring out exactly what items your shop will make and sell, make sure that you're setting yourself up to be an expert on at least those items. Developing a conceptual menu several months prior to your opening can help you to make sure you understand the intricacies of everything you intend to sell.

Choosing your beans

Good beans are the first ingredient for any successful coffee shop. Deciding whether you want to buy green beans and roast them or buy pre-roasted beans is the first menu choice you have to make. Roasting in-house significantly lowers your per-pound cost, but it does require more space and the roasting equipment itself will be a large up-front investment. You will also need someone who is able to roast the beans consistently, which can complicate matters for a new owner-operator.

If you're roasting your own beans in-house, this means deciding how you want to source your beans. Look up the green coffee distributors who make deliveries in your area. Consider whether you want to offer a range of different options, or whether you want to focus on a certain geographical area. Also consider whether it's important that your beans be Organic, Fair Trade, or Rainforest Alliance Certified. Beans that carry these labels will cost a bit more, and you may find yourself more limited in regions and varieties that you can offer.

If you're serving pre-roasted beans, you'll be best-served by ordering them through a local roaster, if one is available. The quantities of beans you'll need just for brewing drip coffee and espresso will be very costly to ship from a far distance, and buying local is also a better way to ensure your beans are fresh when they

27

reach you. Most roasters will set up a free cupping for you if you tell them you're opening a coffee shop and interested in serving their beans. If you live in an urban area, you should have no trouble finding a few nearby coffee roasters to choose from; if you're in a smaller area, your choices may be more limited.

Coffee drinks

With very few exceptions, modern coffee shops offer at least two brewing methods: drip and espresso. The drip brew will be for your standard coffee of the day and au laits, while an espresso machine allows you to offer everything from simple lattes and Americanos to more specialized drinks like cortados and flat whites.

Other brewing methods that you offer beyond this are purely optional but are getting more and more common in modern coffee shops. You may hear about places that have a "slow bar." This generally refers to a separate counter where customers can get methods that take longer to brew, typically pour-over and Chemex. It's also not uncommon for shops to offer French presses; individual French presses that customers can take back to their tables can be a fun touch for a coffee shop aimed at people who want to sit and study.

When it comes to drinks like lattes and cappuccinos, the coffee itself is only half of the equation. You'll also need to think about what milk and flavoring choices you'll offer. Most modern shops will, at a minimum, offer whole milk, skim milk, and at least one non-dairy option. Soy is the most popular, though almond and hemp are gaining ground. When it comes to adding flavors, most shops will at minimum offer chocolate (for hot chocolates and mochas) and vanilla (for lattes). You can find bottled syrups in an incredible range of flavors; Torani and Monin are two popular brands. It is becoming more common for artesian coffee shops to offer house-made syrups instead of pre-bottled varieties. Like with roasting your own beans, these give you a lower per-ounce cost and offer more customization of the flavorings themselves, but is more time-intensive.

Other beverages

Not everyone who comes into your shop will be looking for coffee. Coffee shops also often offer tea, juices, and sodas. Hot tea is an easy item to add to your menu. You can also consider offering tea lattes, which have been growing in popularity in recent years. The chai tea latte is the best-known of these, but London Fogs and Matcha lattes (made from powdered green tea) can be seen on more and more coffee shop menus across the United States.

If you already have syrups on hand for coffee drinks, offering Italian sodas is as easy as buying bottles of club soda. Bottled or fountain sodas can also be an option. Making your own juices in-house can be a bit more of a hassle since it will require some specialized equipment, but can be a relatively easy way to differentiate yourself from the competition if fresh juices aren't common in your area.

Food options

Most coffee shops will offer something in the way of food. The main decision you must make is whether you want to prepare the food in-house or order it from a local restaurant or bakery. If you prepare any food in your coffee shop, you'll need to follow much more rigid regulations in regard to health inspection and food safety. You will also need to invest in more kitchen equipment and will need a larger space to accommodate it.

Ordering food from vendors saves you the trouble of preparing it yourself. It does often mean you have less control over what options you offer and will cost you more per item, but the trade-off is well worth it if you want to focus on the coffee side of things. Research potential food vendors in your area. If they have a brick and mortar shop, go there to sample a variety of their options. Pay attention to what's being served in other coffee shops in your city, too; if you find something you really like, look them up and check out what else they offer. Tasting the food is important, but also check out their delivery options, order minimums, and other contract details to make sure they'll work with your business.

As far as what kinds of foods you sell, your options are completely open. Most coffee shops carry baked goods, both breakfast foods like muffins and scones and more dessert-style options like cookies and pies. You may also want to offer light savory fares, like sandwiches and salads. Whatever food you offer, make sure you strike a good balance between offering enough variety and not having a lot of waste. Frozen options that you can put out a few at a time may work better for you in the early stages of the shop than fresh goods, at least until you know roughly how many you should expect to sell a day.

Influence of location

The importance of location in the success of your concept cannot be overstated. There are two ways to approach the relationship between the menu and the location. You can either come up with a concept that's relatively set and look for the best neighborhood for it to thrive, or you can tweak the proposed menu to suit the area once you find a home for your shop.

Space concerns are one factor in this. If you plan to roast your own beans in-house, you'll need to obtain a building that's large enough to accommodate commercial roasters and has adequate ventilation—the roasting process can produce a lot of smoke, especially if you're going with a darker roast.

What kind of customers will frequent your coffee shop is a factor of the location, too. If your concept is centered around latte art or manual brewing, you don't want to put your shop in a business park or other area where the customers are likely to be in a hurry and just want a cup of coffee. A spot near a college campus or shopping district might be a better place for a concept aimed at customers who want to sit and enjoy their beverage in-house.

Finally, looking at what options already exist to customers in the area might induce some changes to your menu and concept. It's not uncommon to see multiple coffee shops sharing the same block, especially in busy urban areas, but in a high-density area, you'll need to pay more attention to what differentiates you from the others. If there's coffee shop three doors down that already roasts their own beans, shifting your focus to making unique bean blends or creating specialty flavors for your coffee and drinks could help you appeal to a slightly different market.

Chapter 4

Branding and Identity

The menu of your restaurant is an important part of what defines your brand, but there's more to your identity as a coffee shop than just the food and drinks you serve. The décor, the atmosphere, and your presence both in the community and on social media will have just as much of an impact on how your coffee shop is perceived by potential customers.

As easy as it is to get excited about your new coffee shop as soon as you start planning, wait to spend any money on anything for your shop until you've ironed out the details of your brand. This includes planning things like your colors, logo, and slogan. If you're not artistically inclined, consider hiring a professional to design your logo. This is the image that will represent your coffee shop in your customers' eyes; it's worth the extra money to make sure it's high-quality.

In many ways, this is the stage of designing your shop that's the most fun because it's when you get to decide, in the big picture, who you are and what you represent. Even if you haven't secured a space yet, sketch out some rough ideas of how you imagine the interior of your coffee shop, and consider how the interior design will reflect your identity.

Remember that just like everything else you come up with before your business opens, your identity doesn't have to be set in stone. Be willing to change details as new information becomes available. Once your coffee shop is open, maintaining a consistent identity is more important for building up your customer base.

Developing a brand

All the advice in the chapter so far has been to develop a concept that you already have in mind. If you don't know what identity you want for your coffee shop, however, that can seem a bit more daunting. If your heart isn't set on any particular style of coffee shop, consider the neighborhood your shop will be in (or the neighborhoods where you're looking, if you don't have a location yet). Think about what they'll look for in their coffee shop experience, and visit other coffee shops in the area to see what kind of experience they offer.

Be wary of starting a coffee shop whose concept is based on a current trend. Keeping up with trends can be helpful for building your customer base and your knowledge of the coffee industry, but trends don't have the same long-term appeal as coffee in general. You may find your customer base waning as the current trends shift, sending you scrambling to change your identity with each shift in the market. Basing your shop's premise around fads also makes it more difficult to build and maintain a consistent core of customers. If an individual trend seems like it would work well for your coffee shop, there's no reason not to embrace it, but try to steer clear of jumping from one trend to the next; this approach will ultimately limit your business' chance of success.

Social media

Online platforms are one of the best ways to reach potential customers in the modern market, and how you construct your social media presence is an important part of your initial marketing. A blog can be a great tool for a coffee shop since it can help you establish yourself as an authority in the field. You can also use it to tell your customers about new coffees or menu items. As far as what other platforms to go with, Facebook's popularity makes it a good choice for any business. Instagram's visual focus makes it a useful tool for a coffee shop, especially if you have a focus on latte art or make your own food. Twitter is also a nice tool because you can use it to promote your posts on other platforms, or simply to share quick thoughts with your customers; since posts are so short, they're easy to put up quickly as you're going about your day.

Posting regularly is the main key to a successful social media strategy. You don't necessarily need to add content every day, but you should establish a regular schedule and stick to it. While each platform has its own core users and will give you access to a different group of potential customers, you should only maintain as many platforms as you can keep up with consistently. Having a well-maintained blog and strong Facebook presence will serve you better than accounts on five different platforms that you only post sporadically.

Chapter 5

Location

The prevailing wisdom when you open any business says that location is arguably the most important single factor in your success. This is especially true when it comes to a business like a coffee shop. There are enough coffee shops already in existence in most areas that, unless you offer something truly unique and special, you shouldn't expect customers to travel very far to get to you. It's more likely that the bulk of your business will come from people who live in the area, work nearby, or are already in the neighborhood because of another attraction.

The ideal location for a coffee shop, in very general terms, is somewhere that's centrally located to a place where people already gather. Consider locations that people will be drawn to throughout the year. Major shopping areas, for example, are great places for coffee shops. People will already be there and may be interested in a coffee shop as a place to sit and rest, even if they're not particularly fond of coffee. Similarly, you can look for places that are close to theaters, museums, sporting arenas, doctor's offices, salons, or schools—anywhere that will draw people in, and all the better if it's a place where people will need to wait for things to start or have time to kill.

While this is a good general rule of thumb, you should also consider your concept and vision if you already have it planned out, and use that to influence where the ideal location is for your business. If your concept is built around having a slow bar, for example, it's probably best to look for a location where people will be in less of a hurry—near a college campus or park, perhaps, rather than in an office park where people will want to get their coffee and go.

While the obvious and visible details of the location you choose are important, equally important are the details of the business side of your operation—things that might not be so obvious to a first-time business owner. Finding a location that was a restaurant, café, or bar in its previous life can save you money in the long run, since you won't need to re-design the interior from scratch. This is a nice perk when it comes to things like counters and display shelves, but is even more key when it means hidden fixtures like pipes for water or gas are already in place exactly where you'll need them.

The physical location might have the most impact when it comes to drawing in customers, but the terms of your lease are just as important from a business perspective and aren't so easily discerned from observational research. Make sure you know exactly what you'll be paying each month, how long you'll be guaranteed to have that rate, how long you're required to remain in the space, and which services or extra charges are included compared to those you have to pay yourself. A location inside a mall might have a higher per-foot monthly rent than one on the street, but if the mall space comes with utilities included, its ultimate cost could be lower than that on the stand-alone space, just to cite one example. Pay attention to the terms of any lease that's presented to you and make sure you understand every aspect of it before you sign. This can ultimately be one of the main factors that will influence your chances of success.

Beyond the terms of the lease you sign, pay attention to the local laws and regulations. Different counties, cities, and neighborhoods can have very different and specific rules when it comes to things like property taxes, sales taxes, and employee regulations. In urban areas, especially, you may find that the rules vary even from one block to the next, if the neighborhood boundaries are particularly convoluted or close together. Certain areas may also have regulations with a more direct impact on your design and operations. Some areas have specific rules about the kinds of signage you're allowed to post outside your business, which can affect how visible you are to your customers. Others may have certain rules about your operating hours or interior design, especially if it's an area that's predominantly focused on commerce and wants to provide visitors with a cohesive experience.

Ultimately, all this advice can be boiled down to one sentence: do your research before you decide so you can be sure you know what to expect from your location. Even beyond the due diligence of looking into local regulations, you should spend some time in the area observing the traffic patterns and scoping out the typical demographic that comes to the area. Talk to the owners of other businesses in the same vicinity, too. Even if they run a drastically different kind of business, they're likely to have some valuable insight into the area's viability, potential problems, and general attitude or atmosphere—insight you won't get from the property manager or mortgage broker you deal with on the business side of things.

Chapter 6

Design

The design of your coffee shop is about more than just what color you want to paint the walls. It includes every physical detail of your space, from the parking lot and landscaping outside your shop to the location of individual furnishings within it. While it might seem like a secondary detail, the design of your shop is very important to your success. Not only does it send a message to your customers about what they should expect to find inside, but it can affect the way both your customers and your employees navigate the space—ultimately something that can make or break your coffee shop.

How much control you have over your shop's design will vary depending on your location. The amount of construction you're allowed to do in your space (and what kind of documents you must file to be allowed to undertake said construction) is something you should find out during the location search phase of your business planning. If you are purchasing your space, you'll mainly need to pay attention to your locality's building code regulations and the exact boundaries of your property, so that you know if things like the parking lot and sidewalks are part of your purview. If you're leasing, pay attention to what you're allowed to alter and what kind of documentation or permission you'll need to get to do so.

When it comes to the design of your shop, adequate planning is the key to preventing yourself from needing to make costly changes later in the process. As soon as you know the basic dimensions of your space you should create a floor plan. You can even begin to sketch out your floor plan before you've obtained your exact location and then tweak it to suit the space you end up in if you want to get a head start on the design phase.

There are several free services that you can access online that allow you to create professional-looking floor plans without drafting experience or artistic skill. The program Autodesk Homestyler is a popular option. You can choose whether you want to design your space from scratch or start with one of the pre-made designs in their gallery and personalize it to suit your needs. RoomSketcher is another viable choice. It has the advantage of using a drag and drop interface that's simple to learn, even for the technologically challenged. While it doesn't have quite as many features as Autodesk Homestyler, it gives you everything you need for basic shop design.

Once you've come up with a floor plan, don't rush to execute it. If possible, have other coffee shop owners review your floor plan to see if there's anything they would change or any potential problems that you've overlooked. Going over it with your construction team before they start the process is also a good idea. It will make sure they know what the big picture looks like before starting in on the details, and gives them a chance to find practical issues you may not have noticed.

If you have the time and resources to do so, insert a design trial phase between the sketch of your floor plan and the final implementation. Go into your physical space with semi-temporary furnishings to represent the major areas of your shop, like the espresso bar, register, and condiment station. If you can get a group of friends together who can take on the roles of employees and customers, that would be ideal; if that's not possible, you can still go through yourself, imagining yourself in both roles, to see where there may be unanticipated problems with traffic or workflow.

It takes time to craft a well-designed floor plan, but the time spent is certainly worth it for the hassle it will save you down the line. Even after you've obtained your location and designed the first draft of your floor plan, be willing to make alterations to it in response to new information. You want your entire shop to be functional no matter what the situation. When it comes to small furnishings, like customer tables, you can adjust as you go, but pay special attention to the placement of larger objects like your main bar area, your register counter, and other permanent fixtures. Moving those after you open will be significantly more of a hassle than if you catch problems in the construction phase.

Customer areas

Traffic management is the main goal you want to achieve when you set up your customer areas. There are three main areas where you'll have to prepare for a back-up in the customer flow: the register, the pick-up area for bar drinks, and the condiment station. You want to make sure that there is space in your shop for customers to form a line for the register without interfering either with traffic through the front door or access to frequently-used areas like the bathrooms. You also want to make sure that your drink pick-up area is spaced far enough away from the register that there won't be confusion as to whether customers are waiting to place their order or grab their drink. When it comes to the condiment station, make sure it's large enough that multiple customers can comfortably dress up their coffee at the same time. It should be conveniently located to both the front door and the main counter while still being out of the main traffic flow.

The location of your main counter and bathrooms is likely to be dictated at least partially by the availability of plumbing fixtures and electrical outlets. If your location was a food service establishment in a past life, it likely already has both genders of bathrooms already in place, and may even have a counter area already installed. Unless there are serious issues with the locations of these existing fixtures, you'll likely find it easiest to design the space around them.

Even if the space has already been used as a restaurant in the past, however, make sure you obtain an up-to-date listing of your area's building codes and confirm that the existing fixtures comply with these regulations. Older businesses may have been grandfathered to allow code violations, so you can't always trust that things are set up correctly. Consider factors like handicap accessibility and the quantity and location of fire exits. These are things that it will be much less expensive to have right from the beginning than to have to re-do down the line in response to a failed inspection.

The arrangement of your seating is also something you want to consider. The exact placement of tables, chairs, and couches can be adjusted easily, but you should think about what customers who want to hang out in your shop will need. Make sure there are sufficient outlets spaced throughout the seating area. Consider the noise levels at various places in your café. Customers who are there to study or work may want to have available seating away from loud appliances like the blender and coffee grinders. Also, consider what kind of seating you want to put in front of windows or close to doors; while these will likely be popular seating locations when it's nice out, they can be less comfortable options during the colder months.

Employee areas

The interior space in a full-service restaurant is divided into two main areas, generally referred to as "front of the house" (or areas accessible by customers) and "back of the house" (areas such as the kitchen and stock rooms, accessible only by the staff). In a typical coffee shop, these lines are blurred slightly since brewing coffee, making drinks, and even most food preparation is done in full view of the customers within the main dining area. Even though the divisions between the employee and customer areas are less strict, however, you will still need to take a different approach to the design.

Whereas the customer areas of your shop should be designed with an emphasis on traffic volume and flow management, the employee areas should be designed for maximum efficiency in the workflow of the baristas. While someone with no coffee shop experience could design a reasonable customer area, you should bring a working barista in to consult on the layout of your employee areas if you haven't worked in a coffee shop before.

In the main work area, the most important thing is for your staff to have easy access to everything that they'll need to perform their designated task. This is most important in the region of the espresso machine. In addition to the espresso machine itself, you'll also want to have easy access to a small milk fridge, a sink for rinsing milk pitchers, and your espresso grinders. A two-group espresso machine is designed for a single user at a time, but if you're using a four-group espresso machine, make sure the space is arranged so that multiple people can work on it at the same time without interfering with each other.

Drinks that don't require preparation beyond pouring are usually best positioned close to your registry so that the barista working this station will be able to take care of them while someone else is making the more complicated bar drinks. This includes drip coffee, hot and iced tea, and any bottled drinks your store offers. Universal fixtures like the hot water tower and ice bin will need to be centrally located to both the espresso bar and register.

Your main shop grinders should be in the same area as your drip brewers or manual brewing stations. You will also either need to have a scale in the same area (for weighing the beans you're going to grind) or have a system in place for pre-portioning the brews. If you also plan to sell whole bean coffee, you will also want to make the grinder and scale easily accessible in this area, or else have a second of each for use with bean retail. Quick food items, like pastries or pre-made salads and sandwiches, are also typically most convenient when stored close to the register; food that requires preparation will need its own area.

Even though most coffee shops don't have a kitchen or other features typically considered "back of the house," you will still want to have an area of the shop that's completely out of the customer's view. This back area is where you'll have your mop sink, three-part sink, dishwasher, main refrigerator and freezer, and stock room. Since coffee shops typically have a smaller staff than most restaurants, it is at your discretion whether you will also need things like a manager's office, break room, or employee bathroom.

You will also need to consider the practical needs of your equipment when you're laying out the employee areas. Most of your largest equipment will require both a water hook-up and electricity to function, including your espresso machine, drip brewers, and hot water tower. Equipment like scales, grinders, and fridges will only need power, but can use a lot, especially when all of them are running at once; ensuring both that enough outlets are available and that they can handle the voltages you'll be using will save you a lot of headaches in the future.

There is no one correct layout for a coffee shop. Studying the set-ups utilized by other shops in your area can certainly help you to get an idea of what works well. Consider a variety of situations. Figure out how many people you'll have working at one time during your busiest periods and make sure that the space is large enough to accommodate them. At the same time, you want to make sure that everything is relatively close together so that fewer staff members can still run the shop effectively during your less busy periods.

Exterior areas

The exterior design of your café won't necessarily affect your day-to-day operations, but it is still a very important thing to consider. The outside of your shop is the first thing your customers will see. Especially when you're first starting out and haven't yet built a reputation, it is very important in conveying to potential customers what they can expect from your coffee shop.

As mentioned in the previous chapter, the extent of the control you have over your exterior design will vary based on the terms of your lease and the regulations in your area. If the sidewalks around your shop are part of your domain, you should make sure they're well-maintained; the same is true of the parking lot if your business has one. Other details you'll want to think about on the exterior of your building are the signage, the landscaping, and the appearance of exterior walls.

Chapter 7

Brewers and Grinders

While the location is widely considered to be the most important single factor in the success of your coffee shop, the equipment you purchase is not far behind it. The quality of your equipment will affect the taste of the coffee you serve and the speed with which you're able to make it. Making sure your coffee shop is equipped with dependable, professional-grade grinders, brewers, and other fixtures will help to make sure you start off with the best possible chance of success.

The equipment you need to purchase will also make up a large percentage of your opening budget. The good news is that, with proper care and maintenance, professional coffee equipment will last well over a decade. If your aim is long-term success, quality equipment is an investment worth making.

Your menu and your anticipated sales volume will be the most important factors in determining what equipment you want to buy. Equipment that can handle high use volume will be initially more expensive but will also require less maintenance and will be cheaper in the long run than buying a sub-par machine that has to be replaced after a year or two. The option with the highest price tag isn't necessarily the best option. Do your research and shop around so you know what you want to buy and how much you should reasonably expect to spend, and get at least two prices for each piece of equipment before you buy.

Much of the more general inventory and equipment you'll need to buy for your shop was already discussed in Chapter 2, but this discussion was focused more on the quantity and price of the items than what to look for when you're making your purchase. The sections that follow in this chapter will go into more detail about the equipment specific to a coffee shop that you'll want to consider most carefully when you're in the preparation stages.

Espresso machine

For most coffee shops, the espresso machine is the heart of the operation. Not only will you use it to prepare most of your customers' drinks, it is also the single most expensive piece of equipment you'll buy. Because of this, you'll want to be sure what brand and style of machine you want before making any purchasing decisions.

The first choice you need to make is what level of automation you want in your espresso brewing. There are four broad categories in the professional espresso machine world: manual, semi-automatic, fully-automatic, and super-automatic. A manual machine gives the barista the most control over the drink. While the boiler is still often controlled with electronics, everything else—including the water pressure, volume, and temperature—is in the hands of the person operating the machine. This may be appealing to an artesian shop with a focus on exceptional espresso preparation but is impractical for a high-volume café. On the other side of the equation, a super-automatic machine does pretty much everything using electronics, including grinding, dosing, and tamping the shots. The barista can control the timing and temperature by programming the machine but not on an individual drink-by-drink basis; drinks are prepared by pushing the appropriate button on the machine's interface. While this makes them easy to use, they're generally not the best choice for most coffee shops. Not only do they tend to produce lower-quality drinks and eliminate your ability to make latte art, most of them can only prepare one drink at a time and have the highest per-group cost of any style of espresso machine.

A semi-automatic or fully-automatic espresso machine is the best choice for most coffee shops. These machines give you a good balance between quality control and ease of drink preparation. In a semi-automatic machine, the water pressure and boiler temperature are automatic, though the barista still controls the length of the brew time. In a fully-automatic machine, the brew length and water volume are also controlled electronically. Most fully-automatic machines also include semi-automatic controls, making them the most versatile option; on the flip side of this, they also tend to be a bit pricier than semi-automatic options.

Once you've decided on the style of machine, your next decision will be how many drinks you want to be able to make at once. A one-group machine will be able to pour two shots at the same time; a four-group machine can pour up to eight shots at once, and often also has two steam wands, meaning two baristas could operate the machine simultaneously. Since many common drinks can use up to four shots, you'll at minimum want to invest in a two-group model. As you may expect, the more groups are on the machine, the more expensive it will be.

Regardless of what style and size of espresso machine you decide on, there are some other details you should look out for, as well. It is imperative that you purchase a dual-boiler machine which will allow you to brew espresso and steam milk at the same time. It's also important that the machine can generate enough pressure to brew quality shots. Anything that's rated 9 bars or over should be plenty for your needs. Most baristas prefer working with a steam wand that has a knob activation instead of an on/off switch or lever since this gives you more fine-tuning options for your milk. Avoid features like frothing aids and crema enhancers, which are useless at best and can often negatively affect the taste of your drinks.

La Marzocco is probably the most popular brand of espresso machine in American specialty coffee shops. DeLonghi, Nuova Simonelli, and Slayer are also excellent brands to check out. Look through the product catalogues of at least a couple brands to see what different features and price points they offer before making your decision. Some companies will even offer to have you visit their headquarters and try out a few models if you tell them you're considering their machine for your shop.

Grinders

You will need two different styles of grinder in your café: commercial all-purpose grinders (often called "shop grinders") and espresso grinders. Commercial grinders give you a range of grind sizes from coarse to very fine, making them perfect for drip brewing, manual brewing, and retail ground coffee. Espresso grinders give you more accurate adjustments within a narrower size range, letting you fine-tune your grind.

In both cases, you'll want to buy a burr grinder that's designed for commercial use. Even high-end home grinders are not designed for the volume of use they'll see in a café, and you'll likely wear out the burrs and burn out the motor in a year or less. You'll find that burrs come in either cylindrical or conical versions. Many people prefer cylindrical burrs because the shape allows gravity to help push the beans through, rather than relying on the burrs to do it, which can generate more friction and heat, causing your grinds to clump.

With espresso grinders, you also have the choice of dosing or doserless models. In a dosing grinder, the coffee that comes out of the burrs is deposited into a dosing chamber, where it's divided into portions which the barista releases with a level. This makes the flow of coffee into the portafilter easier to control, for a more even distribution. On a doserless grinder, the ground coffee is released straight into the portafilter. This means they're often messier and require more barista control. Modern doserless grinders do often give you the option to program how much coffee you want it to release in each shot, which can cut down on waste.

You will want to have two espresso grinders so that you can seamlessly switch between regular and decaf. How many shop grinders you need depends on your plans for the shop. Lower-volume operations can get away with a single shop grinder. If you want to sell retail ground beans or do manual brewing, however, having two will be more convenient.

Other equipment

Commercial drip brewers are a necessity for the vast majority of coffee shops. Drip coffee typically makes up between 25% and 30% of a coffee shop's sales, making it an important piece of equipment to have. You want a brewer that can make 1-gallon batches quickly, and that can keep the coffee hot until you're ready to serve it without affecting the taste. Your anticipated volume will tell you how many brewers you need. There are 128 ounces in a gallon. In terms of drinks, that's 16 8-ounce pours, 10 12-ounce pours, or 6 20-ounce pours. Using urns that can keep the coffee hot off the brewer will let you keep up with the morning rush without as many brewers, but you will still likely want at least two, and as many as four.

A blender is a piece of equipment that most coffee shops must consider, as well. The market has been steadily growing for blended coffee drinks. Having a blender also allows you to make non-coffee drinks like smoothies and juices. Like with grinders, don't expect a home kitchen blender—even a high-quality one—to be able to keep up with a café's volume. You should only need one, so if you're going to offer blended drinks, it's best to pay the money to do it right.

There has also been a trend in recent years toward offering more brewing methods than simply espresso and drip. The good news about adding these items is that the equipment you need for them is relatively inexpensive. Chemex brewers, French presses, pour-over cones, and other manual brewing methods usually cost between $10 and $50 a piece, depending on the size. Determining how you're going to arrange your behind-counter space to accommodate other brewing methods will be a bigger question than whether they'll fit into your budget.

Chapter 8

Making It Official

The design and concept side of setting up a coffee shop is the fun part, but before you can open your doors there are also some legal procedures you'll have to go through. The specifics vary greatly from city to city. Your local Small Business Association or Chamber of Commerce will be an excellent resource for figuring out exactly what you need to do to operate a business legally in your locality.

There are other things that aren't required but still may be something to investigate. Establishing an LLC for your company, for example, will help you to keep your work finances and personal finances separate. You'll need to set up some kind of legal structure for your coffee shop so that you'll be able to do business as your company, rather than as yourself. This also allows you to take important steps like opening a business bank account.

Some of the other most important things you'll need to do prior to opening your doors are discussed below. Start looking into these regulations as soon as you have your location, ideally several months before opening. You want to schedule your inspections far enough in advance of opening day that you have time to make any necessary changes.

Registering Your Business

Registering the name of your business will allow you to do things like open a bank account in its name, and is an important step before you can open. Registering as a legal entity will also prevent other businesses from operating under the same name in your state. Each state has slightly different rules on how to do this; your local government offices should have some information on how it works in your location. You may also have to separately register your Doing Business As name before you can move forward legally with your business.

If you will have employees in your shop, you will also need to obtain a federal tax ID, also referred to as your EIN (Employer Identification Number). You want to wait to do this until you're ready to open your shop, however, because you'll have to start paying estimated taxes for your business as soon as you've obtained one. Individual states often also have steps you have to take to register with their tax authorities.

Health and building codes

Before you'll be allowed to open for business, you will need to have your building inspected by the city. You will need to wait until you have your equipment installed for the health inspector to come, though the building inspector may be able to come earlier and check out fixtures like plumbing, electrical wiring, and fire safety measures, to ensure they're all up to code. Some states have rules about how far in advance of your opening you need to have these inspections scheduled. Even if they don't, it's generally a good idea to schedule the inspections as early as you possibly can. If anything is found that's not up to code, you'll need to fix it before you open, and you want to leave yourself time to do that without having to push your grand opening back.

Get a copy of the health and building codes as soon as you've picked out your location, even if it will be a while before you're ready to schedule inspections. Tailoring your business to meet these guidelines as you go will mean less time and money spent correcting errors in the future.

Insurance

If you have employees, you will need to get Worker's Compensation insurance. Beyond being the law, this is simply a good idea, protecting you and your staff in case someone gets injured on the job. Some states also require you to have additional protection, so make sure you look into what's required before starting to shop around.

In addition to insuring your workers, you will also need to ensure your business itself. General Liability Insurance is a good idea for any company that works regularly with customers. It protects you from lawsuits if someone besides an employee gets injured on your property and helps with other liabilities. You should also get Property Insurance to protect your café and all the equipment from theft or damage.

Chapter 9

Day-to-Day Operations

After all the work you've done to prepare for your opening day, it can be a bit overwhelming to realize that your hard work has only just begun. Now it's time to run the company that you've spent months or even years conceptualizing and building. While it's difficult to know exactly what your business' daily operations will look like until you're doing it, preparing ahead of time for what to expect can help you to work smarter, and to build your café's sales and reputation more quickly.

As the owner, the standards that apply to the entire business will come from you. The staff will look to you to lead the way on matters like quality, cleanliness, and the right attitude to take in interactions with customers and coworkers. A café owner should be the best barista in his or her shop, and the most knowledgeable about the equipment, menu, and ingredients. This is especially important toward the beginning of your café's life when your staff is small, and your daily sales are more difficult to predict.

The sections below discuss some aspects of your day-to-day operations that you should make decisions on before opening your doors. Developing a system for things like training and placing orders can help make sure important details don't get lost in the shuffle while you're dealing with the daily challenges of your business.

Hours of operation

Perhaps the first decision you need to make is on what days and at what times your coffee shop will be open for business. The busiest hours of most coffee shops are in the morning, typically between the hours of 7 a.m. and 9 a.m. on the weekdays and a bit later (8 a.m. to 10 a.m.) on the weekends. In a recent study, two-thirds of daily coffee drinkers stated they consumed their first cup within an hour of waking up. Consider your location and your target demographic carefully when determining your operating hours; you won't get much business if you're not open when your customers need you.

A café in a residential neighborhood has the highest probability of serving customers that first cup of their day and will want to open early enough to do so. You may want to open your doors as early as 6 a.m. to catch early risers. Making your café a community hub can be a great way to build a loyal customer base. This often means extending your hours into the evening, when people will be hanging out after they've gotten off work, as well as staying open on the weekends.

In a business district, you'll probably get the most business when people are on their way to work, with smaller rushes at lunchtime and in the early evening. You'll want to open no later than 7 a.m. to catch early commuters, and by 6-7 p.m. you will have done most of your sales for the day. You may even want to close on the weekends in this kind of setting or maintain shortened hours.

In a shopping or recreational district, you'll likely want to maintain longer operating hours than a café in an office park. You will likely have the highest per-hour sales in the morning, but the flow of customers will be generally more consistent throughout the day, with peaks at the lunch hour and in the early evening. Pay attention to what businesses are in your immediate vicinity. If you're next-door to a theater, you may get more customers before and after shows; if you're surrounded by restaurants, you might have more of a spike in sales during dinner hours. Your busiest days are likely to be the weekends, and you'll most likely want to maintain evening hours, staying open as late as the shops around you.

Your operating hours and staffing needs are obviously closely linked. If you plan to be the sole employee of your business when you first open, you'll need to make sure you have time to take care of the behind-the-scenes work involved in a café—things like going to the bank, placing orders, taking inventory, and paying bills. This may mean closing early one day of the week, so you can make deposits before the bank closes, or closing for an hour in the afternoon so you can run errands in the middle of the day. If you are the sole employee, you should not plan to be open for more than eight hours a day and should consider closing one day every week to give yourself a day off. The early months of owning a new business can be challenging, and you don't want to burn yourself out before you even have a chance to get rolling.

Staff

Having even a small staff can greatly improve the functioning and efficiency of your coffee shop. Finding the right staff is one of the biggest challenges that most small businesses face. You need people that are reliable, trustworthy, and skilled—people you can count on to be the face of your business when you're not there.

A good rule of thumb is to hire slowly, and only as needed. If you've worked before in the coffee industry in your city, you probably have a few friends who'd be willing to pick up a shift or two at your coffee shop while you're first getting started. As your business gets more consistent, you can hire people on a more regular, full-time basis.

Figuring out how many staff members you need to run your shop can be a tricky matter in and of itself. Once you're open, you can track your cup count, or how many individual drinks you made in a given span of time; this tends to be a more accurate indicator of your relative business than the check count. Some drinks will take longer to make than others. A cup count of 30 per hour means the barista had an average of two minutes per drink—a reasonable amount to expect a well-trained barista to handle on their own. For a cup count higher than 30 per hour, you should plan on having at least two staff members on duty: one to run the register and pour simple drinks while the other works the espresso machine and any manual brewing methods.

Identify which hours you need to have more than one person working based on your cup count, as well as how much time you'll need to spend doing work away from the counter in a given week. Add both to the total number of hours your business is open in a given week, then add an additional 1-2 hours per operating day for opening and closing procedures.

The number that you get is the total amount of staffing hours that you need per week. Most small coffee shops will need between 100 and 150 staff hours in a given week. The owner will often work between 40 and 60 of those hours in a given week, meaning you'll want to supplement with a small staff of between two and six other baristas.

Hiring is no easy feat, and even people who have been business owners for decades can sometimes struggle to find the right staff. When you can, it's often best to hire for attitude and personality. Experience in a coffee shop can be a plus, but you can teach someone to pour an espresso shot much more easily than you can teach them to be friendly with customers. No matter how well the person does in the interview, you don't really know how well someone will fit on your staff until they've worked a few shifts on the floor. If someone you hire is hurting the business, don't hesitate to let them go.

Inventory management

Being able to correctly manage your inventory means never running out of the things you need while still avoiding waste of perishable items. Having a system to track your inventory is a necessity. Some POS systems come with an inventory management tool included, and there are stand-alone options you can either purchase or download for free, but you can use something as simple as a running spreadsheet on a tablet, as long as it enables you to track your inventory successfully.

For every item you use frequently, you should establish a set of pars. This is how much of an item you want to order up to, that will get you comfortably to your next order date without having too much left over. Before you place each order, count the amount of the item you have in the inventory, then subtract that from your par. The number that results is how much you need to order. With non-perishable items, you can set the pars as high as you have space for; with perishable goods, the pars should take you right up to your next order cycle, without having a lot left over.

In addition to your pre-order inventory, about once a month you should inventory everything in your coffee shop, from the pastries in your display case to the boxes of spare cups in your stockroom. While you're going through your stock, you can double-check the dates to make sure they're being properly rotated and make sure you don't need to order anything you don't usually think about, like ceramic cups and extra cleaning products. Maintaining a monthly inventory can also be a good way to keep track of your stock and make sure there's no theft happening in your business. If you seem to be using more product and your sales haven't gone up, that's a sign there's something fishy going on behind the scenes.

As you figure out which vendors will be supplying which of your products, you can determine your order schedule with each of them and come up with systems for tracking and maintaining all the various products you'll stock and use. Having a system in place as soon as possible will prevent you from forgetting orders, and will make it possible for someone else to take care of placing orders in your stead so you won't need to be in the shop every day.

STARTING YOUR OWN COFFEE SHOP

Chapter 10

Marketing

Providing a high-quality experience to your customers is the best way to keep them coming back. If you serve good coffee in a comfortable atmosphere, people will want to visit your café and will tell their friends to go there, too. This kind of word of mouth advertising can be some of the most effective, but when you're first opening your shop you'll probably need to do a little bit more to let people know that you exist. Traditional media advertising methods have largely been replaced by social media for new businesses because it can be more affordable and easier to target to a specific demographic, but these also have their pitfalls and challenges. A combination of approaches is the best way to catch the most customers.

Whether or not you choose to have a strong presence on social media outlets like Facebook or Twitter, one thing you should absolutely do for your business is set up a website. This will help your customers know where to find you and what to expect from the experience. If you do use other social media outlets, your website can serve as the hub and landing page for your online presence. You may even want to have an attached store for selling whole beans or branded products. You can use a service like WordPress to set up a website for free, but if you want full customization options it's worth the money to pay for a more comprehensive service.

You want to begin your marketing efforts before you even open your doors. If you can get your customers excited for you to open, this will generate buzz that has people talking about your shop from day one. Building your website should be a part of this, as should posting on your chosen social media outlets, but don't ignore the possibilities of more traditional marketing approaches, either. You could print up some promotional fliers with a coupon for a free coffee and hang them on doors in your neighborhood, or distribute them at local offices. Offering free samples of what you offer can be a great way to draw in business. You could your time and coffee to run a booth at a community festival or other event, generating goodwill around your name while you're making your would-be customers aware of your presence. On a smaller scale, you could take to-go boxes of coffee to shops and businesses in your area to say hello and invite them to stop in. If you want to go for a more community-oriented vibe in your coffee shop, these more personal marketing approaches will help to grow your business and build your brand all at the same time.

Networking can also play a big role in generating more business for your shop. Join your local Chamber of Commerce or Small Business Association. Along with getting your name out there in your local business community, this is also a great way to learn information and pro tips from people who already run their own businesses. Collaborations with local businesses can help to increase your visibility to their customers. While it's helpful to get to know other coffee professionals in your area, don't limit yourself to people in your industry. If you stay open to a diverse array of marketing opportunities, you'll be more likely to draw a diverse customer base to your shop.

Chapter 11

Turning a Profit

Anyone who's getting ready to open a business has no doubt heard the terrifying statistics of how many fail in their first year. Opening your coffee shop is only your first challenge. Being able to maintain sustained success and turn your coffee shop into a profitable business takes determination, perseverance, and a smart approach to managing your company's financials.

The first thing you need to understand to run a profitable business is the idea of cash flow. This term refers to how much revenue your company generates compared to how many expenses it pays over the same period. In short, it means you're bringing in more money than you're spending across your entire business, not simply whether you're making a profit on your daily sales. Over half of small businesses that end up failing are profitable when they go under. The problem is that they're cash flow negative; they're spending money faster than they're making it, and their business fails as a result.

Managing your cash flow is not easy. It means paying close attention to the overall financial health of your company and budgeting for unanticipated expenses, like equipment failures. After you've tallied up all your anticipated monthly expenses, it's a good idea to tack an extra 10% onto it and make that your profit goal to stay cash flow negative. If you don't end up making any extra expenses, that money can go toward paying other costs associated with your business in the future.

Pricing

How you set your prices will have a big impact on how much profit you're able to generate. How much flexibility you have with your pricing will ultimately depend on your location. Some areas will be more price-sensitive, especially if you're in a particularly dense coffee market.

While it's important to pay attention to what your competitors charge, a data-based pricing method will make sure you're able to cover all your expenses and earn a true profit. Consider your food costs, labor costs, and other operating costs, not only what you're paying for the ingredients. The average food cost for a coffee shop is 15%--in other words, what you spend on food should only equal about 15% of your total sales. You can use this as a rough guide to help you set prices.

The Four Walls Theory

It can be very frustrating when your business isn't turning a profit like you feel like it should. Especially with a densely-populated industry like coffee, it is tempting to blame the problem on factors that are outside your control. Most business owners, though, ascribe to the Four Walls Theory: that most of the time that a business struggles the problem is something within the "four walls," or inside the business.

Competition from other coffee shops, changes in the traffic flow due to construction, or other factors that are beyond your control are easy things to blame problems on. Even if they are the cause of your slow sales, though, you'll do yourself no favors by assuming one of these factors is the cause. If something is outside of your control that means you can do nothing to fix it. If you instead look for things within your business that can be improved, you'll be able to take active steps toward addressing your issue. Even if they weren't the direct reason your sales were low, improving your business will inevitably improve your customer satisfaction, which will in turn naturally improve your profit margins.

Identifying problems within your business can be tricky, especially if you don't have a lot of experience in the industry. Paying attention to customer feedback—whether it's given to you in person or left on a review site like Yelp! or TripAdvisor—can be a significant benefit in homing in on your business' short-fallings. Make sure you keep an eye on your waste and loss figures, as well, and keep tabs on all the payments made from your company's bank account. It's hard enough keeping a small business afloat without having someone dipping into your profit unexpectedly.

Ultimately, a coffee shop is successful when it provides customers with a unique and pleasant experience. If you're struggling to improve your sales, consider how you can better do that. What changes can you make to the menu, atmosphere, or service in your shop that would give the customer more value out of their interactions with you? Keeping your customers at the front of your thoughts whenever you're considering changes to the business is the best way to find the path to success.

One Last Thing!

As an independent author I have a limited budget for promoting my books, so word of mouth is very important for me. You can help me tremendously by leaving a review on Amazon. You have no idea how much this would help!

I also want to give you a one-in-two-hundred chance to win **a $200.00 Amazon Gift card** as a thank-you for reading this book. All I ask is that you give me some feedback, so I can improve it :)

Your opinion is super valuable to me.

It will only take a minute of your time to let me know what you like and what you didn't like about this book. The hardest part is deciding how to spend the two hundred dollars!

Just follow this link.

http://booksfor.review/coffeeshop

Want to

supercharge

your coffee knowledge?

Turn this page...

Also available by

Jessica Simms

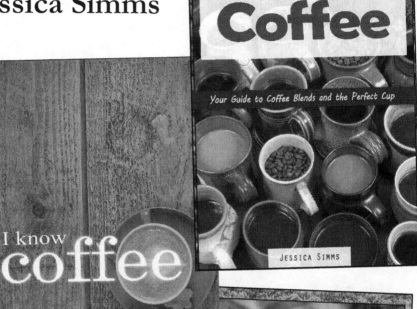

Blending Coffee

Your Guide to Coffee Blends and the Perfect Cup

JESSICA SIMMS

I know coffee

Harvesting,
Blending,
Roasting,
Brewing,
Grinding,
& Tasting
Coffee

JESSICA SIMMS

Harvesting Coffee

Life of a Coffee Bean from Planting to Processing

JESSICA SIMMS

Roasting Coffee

How to Roast Green Coffee Beans like a Pro!

JESSICA SIMMS

Brewing&Grinding Coffee

How to Make Good Coffee at Home

JESSICA SIMMS

Tasting Coffee

Coffee Cupping Techniques to Unleash the Bean!

JESSICA SIMMS

Steaming Milk

Want that Perfect Latte or Cappuccino?

JESSICA SIMMS

The
I know coffee
series

Made in the USA
San Bernardino, CA
01 December 2018